Acknowledgements.....

Dedicated to your kindness

Odd

Deliberations

notions......

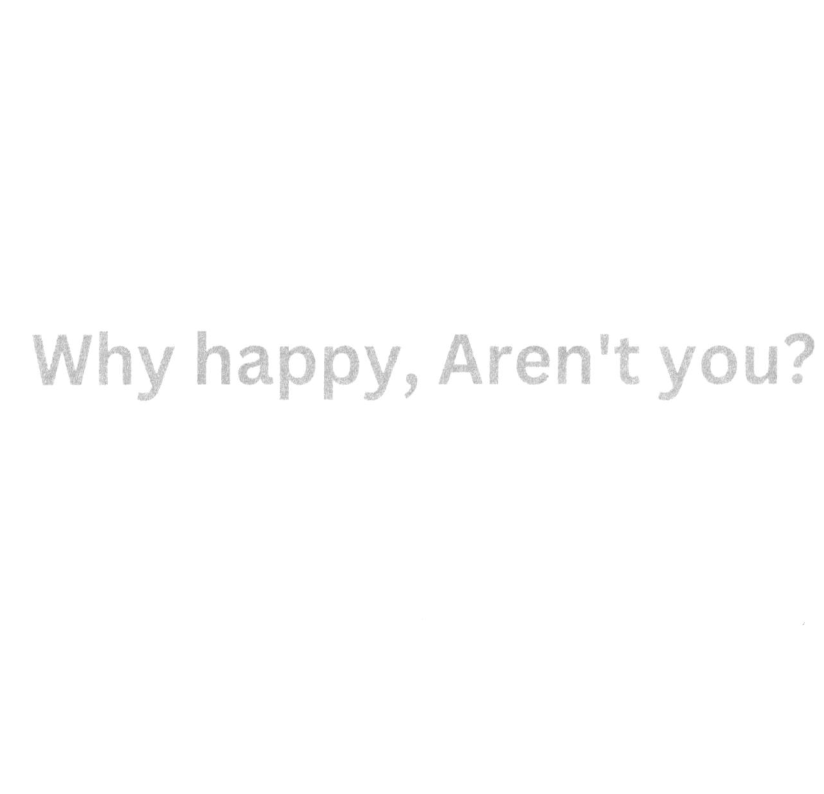
Why happy, Aren't you?

The Sky is blue.
This might not be true

But still, if it is a little true
Then, why Happy, Aren't you?

Midst so much,
That sunlight can't reach the negligible rule

I wander as a true finder,
But, can't even find the roots

"Problems are so much"
Yeah, unfortunately its true

Still, Journey is forever
Why happy, aren't you ?

Master of thoughts

Beyond the desire of this broken world.
Lived a boy who was never told.

"He could do but only if he thought to.
Could achieve anything. if he wants to."

Always thought "I am not gonna make it. not good enough"
"There's millions at the pinnacle."

I don't know but everybody knows.
"how's it done and how it's not."

Petrifying nightmares haunts me a lot.
Is there no one I can trust the most?

Soon. Is the culmination of my life
Soon. I am gonna be lost

And soon enough an elder approached.
Said the wisest he could think the most.

O 'son O 'my child
Don't think a lot.
This hidden world is full of lies and odds

You are not bad. you are
just too good for this world.
Filled with fake desires and cursed dunce.

Apex is far beyond the doors.
Just be the
MASTER OF YOUR THOUGHTS.

Bliss of Intimacy

Love, As the word it says,
I think I found its definition on your charming face.

Feeling is inevitable,
I can't explain.
It is not meant to be sentenced in one phrase.

Pleasurable reactions in mind are invited,
Just imagining about you makes me feel delighted

I am unfortunately obsessed with someone,
I hope this isn't a troll,
Are there any emotions I can control?

Unforgettable is love,
Unforgettable is faith,
Unforgettable are your spoken phrase,
But, at last,
You are someone my mind can never erase.

Mind is confused,
Heart is controlled,
Thoughts are invincible,
My peace is yours.

I always thought of my life as a secrecy.
Until I found you, who resembled bliss of intimacy.

Cloaked Heart

Thou shall not trust.
Thou shall not hurt.

In thy two vivacities,
happens to have a grateful curse of all

Love is what they say.
'Can't live without each other' is what they
pray.

Is it really worthwhile to fall in love?
Accepting this fake world,
being with someone who is not even sure of
the curve.

Sometimes, I imagine to suffer the non
accessible fate
But,
I assume it's more fake than this handwritten
phrase.

Love has its consequences.
so
do you have condolences?

I am not a normie talking about fate.
Take me as a result of all the hate.

Thee should say yourself a Cloaked Heart.
If you've been through enough Darce.

Far from You

Midst of sadness cannot feel my sorrow,
Is there any wisdom I can borrow?

Flatters hit me with the shining thought of thee,
Thou remind me of The Eternal tree

Astoundingly standing without any care,
Admiring sheep thinking of shepherd's gear

Yah, I know I am far from you
Still, when I am lonely, I think of you

Voice of yours, hit the temple
Metting with the pleasure off record
Establishes the peace of mind which
couldn't even a broken record

Yeah, desperation occurs when I even
imagine we are apart,
Beside the boundaries, it unlovingly
touches the heart.

Parallel to our daily natter and chuckling
thee,
I really don't want to envisage that I am far
from you.

Fragmentary Silence

"It's a poem based on history of
'Black gang'
also known as fire strokers who
used to
put coal in furnaces of old ships
during Steam age.
They worked under unhealthy
circumstances.
This poem signifies their risky
work under low wages and low
profile,
and how it's unfair"

"Silence" thy word it says
Peace of mind is its case.

"Exceptional" O' thy blunder
Is it really pleasure or a sham
It's what truth says
not a lad.

Before I continue,
I mean no Hate,
Let's start the year just with a convenient debate.

Ship with hundreds of vilipenders,
commanding the thousands of poor.
Filling Incinerators with fuel dusk,
Attaining problems of lifetime rust.

Tackling low wages with heavy pains,
Was the silence never something for their gain?

Lucky one's above with high acquaintance,
Was the friendly environment only for their presence?

Being called luxury and silence is a bad one,
Partial Silence is a better term.

In this cruel world,
"Peace" is termed "eternal silence"
No matter cruel transfix.

Stronger hurts weaker for hedonism,
and they call it pacificism.

This world is cruel and charged with unacceptance,
Being partial cruel is the only way of subsistence.

WHAT DO YOU REALLY WANT?

Since childhood we are stamped off record,
What they expect from us and what they want.

Our interests?
They mean nothing.
Think for real,
Is this really called affectionating.

Hard truth?
It hurts the most.
Your feelings?
They are off coast.

Remember the moments?
When you laughed like a giggling goose?
Many were behind that emotional truce.

Our overlearning life is not easy as it says,
Behind the fake smile, you can spot the sorrowful face.

"What you really want?"
A question never asked.
Beyond the societies' desires,
lives a never-ending Darce

Goof off with infatuation

Goof off with infatuation,
Go, hustle with your brain's misconceptions.

Merely a truth on the face,
Filled with fake desires and
Dreadful Solace.

'Attraction' a context meant to be ruined,
Faded loyalty and never asked pursuits.

'Are you the really one?'
A riddle unsolved.
Keep in mind,
even roses have thorns.

Calamity of heart,
is thy rapture.
If thou hath even a little sense,
would've focused more on venture.

Starvation of power

Blessing of knowledge,
Blessing of power.
Both are commodities.
We want to devour!

Sometimes it's a must,
Sometimes its faith,
Sometimes a real waste.

Can't reach the destination?
Stop throwing stones at every barking dog.
You are someone,
Who's going to win at any cost.

Obstacles are meant to be,
Success is unreachable,
if you are dead to thee.

Fortune to success?
Highly Misconceptional!
Fortune is something incredibly exceptional.

Not always goes as planned,
Not always as u want.
Its beyond you,
You have to break the record!

Exceeding your limits?
A pleasurable case.
Making it a habit?
A charmful grace.

At the culmination,
I would like to proceed.
Starvation of power,
Is meant to be "keen on" indeed.

Angels and Devils of Mind

In thy souls lies the suppositional world,
Observing the bicker of two vital vivacities

Grufeling are the remains of their knowledge,
Famelicose for the imperishable demands

Severance of their notions leads to infuriation,
Exasperation of minds leads to ramshackle

Divergent outlooks are glee in curse indeed
Upskill the ventures in a charming greet

Innards become virtuoso not - to - mention,
One enlightens the pathway to triumph,
Other instructs the negligence of Inattention

Despite, Transcending the forces of pessimism
They both teach a thing
"How to take and how to give"

In the culmination I would like to postulate
"Both are irrevocable, Liberation is their immutable fate."

Bad Chapters

Life is a book,
Every new chapter with new intentions,
Endless full stops and inevitable misconnections.

Everyday a new chapter,
With charming progress and sorrowful factors.

Some signifies success,
Some signifies a desperate cold,
Some a dreadful threshold.

We can't change what is written, neither see.
Thus, this is a reason why life is entirely called a 'Beauty'.

Each of the lives have different authors
as they say,
Only truth knows what lies beyond that neverendingly highly grace.

Full stops and recaps hurts a lot,
A conclusion is in upper thoughts.

Clear the mind with peaceful thoughts,
So the apex would not be far beyond.

Being successor of the story is must,
Your spark can only light a room,
filled with dark dusk.

Feel the power of every component
around you,
so,
Even Bad Chapters can accept your
gratitude.

Stiff Wretched

Snitch catch,
Nothing had

An inactive lad on the bad,
Thinking of sorrowful dreads.

Doesn't know,
Thou is one in decile
Utterly more than versatile.

O' wonder If there was someone,
there waiting for thee.
Would've focused more on major dews,
than minor truce.

Sadness into anger,
Stiff wretched,
No one cares, even it's too bad.